sport snaps
mike eisenbath

Mark McGwire

the power hitter

25

To my wife, Donna, and our children:
Jessica, Joshua, Erin and Kara.

M.E.

PHOTO CREDITS:

Allsport
8 [V. Laforet], 10 [E. Shaw], 14 [V. Laforet],
20 [V. Lovero], 30 [O. Creule], 33 [K. Cohlen],
34 [O. Creule], 35 [O. Creule], 36 [D. Smith],
37 [O. Creule], 39 [A. Lyons], 45 [M. Stockman],
55 [B. Bahr].

Associated Press
3 [J. Finley], 6 [N. Ninuzzo], 7 [A. Sancetta],
9 [E. Reinke], 42 [T. Tribble], 48 [A. Sancetta],
51 [E. Reinke], 54 [J. Finley].

USC Sports Information
22, 24 [R. Stewart], 26.

USA Baseball
29.

William Greenblatt / United Press International
Front cover, 1, 4, 5, 12, 13, 17, 18, 40, 43, 44, 46,
47, 49, 50, 52, 56.

Hal Hanstein
16.

**Mike Eisenbath's photo courtesy
of Bill Greenblatt.**

Printed by Pinnacle Press, Inc.
in the United States of America.

Edited by Carla Babrick.

Designed by Werremeyer | Floresca.

LIBRARY OF CONGRESS
CATALOG CARD NUMBER 00-107909

table of contents

the days

MARK McGWIRE WILL NEVER FORGET

Ah, there were many days in the 1998 season that Mark McGwire will carry in his heart and memory for as long as he breathes. He clearly had the time of his life.

But there were two days from the Summer of Power, his record-smashing 70-home-run season, that anyone who witnessed the moments at Busch Stadium in St. Louis will recall with a certain fondness and distinct thrill. One registered as something personally special to McGwire; the other made incredible history for baseball — and indeed, for America.

On September 7, 1998, John McGwire celebrated his 61st birthday by watching his son play first base for the Cardinals. Mark hadn't gone shopping for his dad. What do you get a man who has been one of your heroes all your life, anyway? Mark is paid well enough to buy plenty of nice things for his father, but money really couldn't buy that truly special gift.

The son came up with quite a treasure. He hit his 61st home run of the season, the home run that tied him with Roger Maris for most ever hit in a single major-league season.

The birthday-gift blast — hit off Chicago Cubs pitcher Mike Morgan — caromed hard off a glass window of the Stadium Club, the restaurant that overlooks left field. It touched off a celebration that included fireworks in the St. Louis sky and congratulations for Mac from Cubs players as he rounded the bases.

But the best was yet to come. Less than 24 hours later, McGwire was driving to the ballpark for another game against the Cubs. This was the final game of the series. It was a late-afternoon contest that would attract yet another full house and several hundred reporters from all over the world. Anyone paying attention could feel the anticipation when they woke up that morning.

All of that was on McGwire's mind as he sped along the highway. Not much later, he found himself holding a microphone while standing on the field in front of the Cardinals' dugout. The game had to be stopped so he could talk to the crowd.

"Yesterday," McGwire said, "doing what I did for my father, hitting my 61st home run on his 61st birthday, I thought what a perfect way to end the home stand, by hitting my 62nd home run for the city of St. Louis and all the great fans. I really and truly wanted to do it here. Thank you, St. Louis."

Truly a storybook moment.

Steve Trachsel was on the pitcher's mound for the Cubs, who led 2-0 in the fourth inning. All season, McGwire had been chasing the record set by Roger Maris of the New York Yankees in 1961. Well, Mac said he wasn't chasing anything or anyone, that he merely was doing what he does as well as he could. But "The Chase," which turned into a race with Cubs right fielder Sammy Sosa also swatting toward history, developed.

And at 8:18 p.m. on September 8, a Tuesday, that chase ended when McGwire lined the first pitch just barely over the wall in left field.

The next several minutes turned into a blur of emotion and joy. He savored his trip around the bases with a slow trot that actually began somewhat comically: McGwire missed first base. Yep, he stepped right around without his foot landing on the bag, forcing friend and first-base coach Dave McKay to implore him to return, which McGwire did with an 'oh, yeah!" kind of look.

"I don't remember anything after that," McGwire would say later. "I was numb. I thought, 'I still have to play the game. Oh, my God, I can't believe this.' It's such an incredible feeling. I can't believe I did it."

McGwire had a unique trip around the bases, as members of the Chicago Cubs didn't act at all like opponents. Cubs first baseman Mark Grace slapped hands with McGwire. Second baseman Mickey Morandini and shortstop Jose Hernandez each shook his hand. Third baseman Gary Gaetti, who had started the season with the Cardinals and become a friend of McGwire, received a salute from Big Mac. Then the two shared a hug. Before trotting the final 90 feet between third base and home, Mac gave third-base coach Rene Lachemann a

"It was **outstanding.**
America is really enjoying this."

PRESIDENT BILL CLINTON ON THE TELEPHONE TO McGWIRE
AFTER THE RECORD-BREAKING HOME RUN NO. 62

forearm bash and then pointed to his parents seated behind the plate and to the sky, to "the Man Upstairs," he later explained. McGwire hugged Cubs catcher Scott Servais before delivering his familiar smashing-fists, punch-to-the-stomach greeting to teammate Ray Lankford.

And then the celebration really picked up steam.

Matthew McGwire, St. Louis' favorite batboy and Mark's son, took center stage as he shyly but exuberantly approached his dad. Mark lifted Matt high into the air as red-and-white streamers floated all around and fireworks loudly placed an exclamation mark on the proceedings. McGwire couldn't stop hugging people as the emotion spread to everyone – his teammates, manager Tony La Russa, Cardinals coaches. He had another hug for Matt, this time punctuated with a kiss.

Soon, Sammy Sosa appeared. He had 58 homers and had been a part of the chase for several months. Something of a bond had developed between the two men, who had gone through so much scrutiny and pressure. Now, Sosa had to be part of the party, had to offer his congratulations. And McGwire hugged him with incredible enthusiasm.

"I don't know how big the Arch is," McGwire said later, in reference to St. Louis' other enormous landmark, "but I feel like the Arch is off my back now."

Connecting with history, McGwire quickly turned a moment of glee into a heart-rending one. He trotted to the box seats and soon was hugging the children, now grown, of the late Roger Maris. They were all too young to know what their dad had gone through when he broke Babe Ruth's home run record in 1961. McGwire showed the respect he had for Maris, the appreciation, and let his children feel the pleasure their dad never did.

Moments later, McGwire spoke to the nearly 48,000 people filling Busch Stadium, saying, "I dedicate this home run to the whole city of St. Louis and all the fans here. Thank you for all your support. It's unbelievable. All my family, everybody, my son, the Chicago Cubs, Sammy Sosa – unbelievable. Class."

A few hours later, McGwire reflected on the events of the day and still had trouble remembering exactly what had happened. "I just hope I didn't act foolish," he said. "But this is history."

MARK McGWIRE profile

BORN:

OCTOBER 1, 1963,
POMONA, CALIFORNIA

FAMILY:

CHILD, MATTHEW

POSITION: FIRST BASEMAN

HEIGHT: 6 FEET, 5 INCHES

WEIGHT: 250 POUNDS

BATS AND THROWS: RIGHTHANDED

EDUCATION: Damien High School in Laverne, California, and University of Southern California.

TRANSACTIONS: Drafted by the Oakland Athletics in the first round (10th player selected overall) in June 1984. Traded to the St. Louis Cardinals for pitchers T.J. Mathews, Eric Ludwick and Blake Stein on July 31, 1997.

MOST INFLUENTIAL PEOPLE: John and Ginger McGwire, Mark's parents, are respected yet humble people in their Southern California community. They made sure that all five of their sons treated all people the same and put forth an honest effort in anything they tried to do.

IN THE WINTER: Mark likes to travel, and in recent years he has spent some offseason time in Hawaii and Australia. Mainly, he likes to pass time with his son, Matthew, since they don't see each other much during the summer. Mark maintains a challenging weight-training program even in the winter months.

IF HE WASN'T A BASEBALL PLAYER: Mark isn't sure what he would be doing, since he knew fairly early during his time at the University of Southern California that he would be a pro ballplayer. He has friends who hold a wide range of jobs, but Mark has been fascinated by his friends who are police officers and firefighters.

FAVORITE BOYHOOD BALLPLAYERS: Even though he and his brothers played all sorts of sports in their youth and occasionally attended Dodgers games, Mark really didn't consider himself a big fan of any particular player. He did admire the talents of some more than others, and those tended to be the power hitters. Among those he enjoyed watching most were Mike Schmidt, whom he passed on the all-time home run list in June 2000, and Dave "King Kong" Kingman.

1973 | hit home run in first Little League at-bat, age 10

John and Ginger McGwire were well known in their community. John was a dentist, called Doc by many. Ginger probably waited on everyone in town at one time or another as she poured soft drinks and popped popcorn at the town park. Her five sons were always busy playing one game or another.

In some ways, Mark seemed the least likely of the five McGwire boys to excel in athletics. Not because he didn't enjoy sports. He got into everything – baseball, football, golf, basketball. But the other McGwire boys were pretty fair athletes, too. Mark, though, was lucky he could see well enough to play. He has 20-500 vision and as a relatively young boy found out he needed to wear glasses because he could only watch TV by sitting really, really close.

"God doesn't give you everything," McGwire said.

Still, there was something about Mark and baseball that seemed special from the beginning. Actually, he played soccer first and didn't start playing baseball until he was 8, after he was talked into playing by a friend in the neighborhood. He played for a couple of years in one league, then at age 10 started playing in an official Little League – where he hit a home run in his first at-bat.

Playing ball as a boy was always about having fun and not about feeling the pressure to win, McGwire has said. He enjoyed playing football and wiffle ball in the circle of the cul-de-sac as much as wearing a uniform and playing in an organized game.

John McGwire never got to play some of the games that his boys played. He contracted polio when he was 7 and was left with one leg shorter than the other. That didn't keep him from playing golf, bicycling and boxing.

"I've always assumed that we were like most families," Ginger McGwire once said, "that we tried to teach our kids the importance of always doing their best, being polite and respecting other people."

That came in handy as Mark entered Damien High School, an all-boys Catholic school that stressed good grades and solid college preparatory work while boasting a fine athletic tradition as well.

Damien has turned out a few memorable athletes. Several alumni have played in the NFL, and the football program once had six players from the same team go to Division I schools on scholarship. Soccer star Ricky Davis played with the New York Cosmos, the St. Louis Steamers and the U.S. National team. Frank Pastore pitched in the big leagues for the Cincinnati Reds.

552

MLB | career home runs: 552

"It really wasn't a place where people went because they had a strong baseball program, though," McGwire recalled.

His first high school, however, was Claremont. Halfway through his freshman year there, he transferred to Damien. At Damien, there was less competition for spots on the teams: he had a better chance of playing on the varsity early.

"When he first came here to look at the school, his dad was with him," said Tom Carroll, then the baseball coach and now athletic director at Damien. "I saw this big old boy walking around – he was tall even then – but he seemed very shy. He always gave me the impression he was not cocky. He kind of kept to himself. Very polite, gentlemanly."

McGwire tried football. Unlike his brother Dan, who went on to play quarterback at the University of Iowa and San Diego State and play in the NFL, Mark just didn't care for it enough to keep playing. He wasn't a bad basketball player, either, mainly because he was tall and skinny.

In time, it was clear he had a gift for baseball. Yet McGwire quit the game for a while as a sophomore in high school. He quit partly because of a pulled chest muscle that prevented him from swinging a bat for a while, partly in frustration that he hadn't made the varsity yet, and also to keep from feeling burned out. "I was tired of playing baseball and I wanted to take a break," he said.

1565

MLB | career hits: 1565

> "He's the kid who, when he played Little League, all the parents called the president of the league and said, 'Get him out of there. I don't want him to hurt my son.'

I had my mom call the National League office to see if she could do it for me."

DANTE BICHETTE, CINCINNATI REDS OUTFIELDER

At that point, the golf coach wooed him onto the team and "he helped them win a league title that year," Carroll said. "I always felt that if Mark wanted to get out of baseball, he could play golf professionally and be really good at it."

But Mark had the heart for baseball. He loved the game and couldn't stay away. It helped that he had an awesome fastball.

"I would have loved to have seen what he would have done if he would have stayed on the mound," Carroll said.

McGwire finally began his varsity baseball career as a junior. "He had a big-league fastball already but nothing to accompany it," high school teammate Randy Robertson once said. "That didn't matter. He'd wow you with his fastball."

That 1980 season, with McGwire and Mike Alexander starring on the mound, the Damien Spartans won the Baseline Conference baseball championship.

Mark started drawing regular attention from the scouts who routinely scoured California diamonds for talent. There was a night when Damien was playing a tournament game in Pomona. A Detroit Tigers scout's radar gun picked up a McGwire fastball at 90 mph, and the scout later suggested to Carroll that the young pitcher could be even better and throw even harder if Carroll would tinker with his pitching motion.

Carroll declined to make the changes. "I wasn't going to mess with him," McGwire's then-coach figured. "He had good control. He was developing a breaking ball. I didn't know enough to mess with him. It was something that was natural for him, something he worked hard for."

The next year, injuries robbed the Spartans of Alexander and the starting center fielder. Another regular quit baseball, preferring to get a job to pay for his car. The team struggled, though McGwire continued to star. He went 5-3 with a 1.90 earned-run average that senior season.

"His senior year, we used him as the designated hitter when he wasn't pitching," Carroll said. "Mark said he could play first base instead of DH. I was worried about him getting hurt. But there was no doubt he needed to be in the lineup for us every day."

One time, McGwire and the Damien Spartans were playing at a northerly-facing diamond at Ralph Welch Fields in the Pomona Elks Tournament. Mark swatted a ball that carried over the infield and over the outfield, landing on the pitcher's mound of the diamond that faced south. The ball rolled to that other field's backstop, probably more than 500 feet from where McGwire had been standing when he hit the ball.

During the summers, McGwire played for the Claremont American Legion team organized by coach Jack Helber. The group raised money and bought an old bus, which the players painted and boarded for a three-week trip to play in Laramie, Wyoming, and Billings, South Dakota as well as Ogden, Utah, and Las Vegas, Nevada.

It was about that time McGwire got the bug to play baseball past high school graduation. And he showed steady improvement as a pitcher. He loved talking baseball with his teammates on those long bus rides and learned a lot from talking with his fellow pitchers.

"It was a good experience just hanging out with the guys," said McGwire, who always loved to laugh and take part in practical jokes. "The camaraderie, the laughing and growing up like that in those summers, that was the best part of those memories."

Even in high school, McGwire struck his teammates as a quiet, humble person who made great demands of himself on the baseball field. He was rather shy, which might have struck some people as arrogance until they got to know him. Then, they could understand he simply was focused on trying to be the best baseball player he could be.

He didn't like to talk about himself or draw attention to himself. When he wasn't named to the local newspaper's all-star team his senior season, he never let on that it bothered him.

It's not that McGwire wasn't a leader. He just didn't do it with words.

1117

MLB | career runs: 1117

 Pops used to say that Mantle hit the ball
as far as anybody he's ever seen.

But I would say that Mac would put up a great argument.

If somebody can hit the ball farther than Mac,
I'd like to have seen him play."

FORMER CARDINALS PITCHER TODD STOTTLEMYRE, WHOSE FATHER,
MEL STOTTLEMYRE, PLAYED WITH MICKEY MANTLE

"Guys would rally around him because of the way he played," Tom Carroll said. "He was a hard worker. I could always use him ... as a role model for others because I could say, 'If you'd work as hard as Mark does–' What separates talented people like Mark from other people with talent is he wasn't afraid to work."

McGwire didn't really work much extra on his hitting. He was a bit of a high school natural, a hitter because he loved to play. Mark batted .359 and hit five homers that final season at Damien. That summer, because of illness, McGwire played only first base for his Legion team and batted .415 with 14 homers.

"I swear to you, though," Carroll said, "that was not the most impressive thing he did as a ballplayer then. He really wanted to pitch. In the games he didn't start for us, he wasn't afraid to come in to finish the game for us in relief if we needed it."

The pro scouts didn't notice his bat. They paid attention to his arm. The Montreal Expos drafted Mark in the eighth round in June 1981 and wanted him to pitch. They offered him a signing bonus of $8,500.

Baseball Tips for Young Players:
STANCE

WHEN WORKING ON A SUCCESSFUL BATTING STANCE, THE MOST IMPORTANT PLACE TO START IS GOOD BALANCE. KEEP YOUR HANDS BACK. TRY TO KEEP YOUR BODY AS "QUIET" AS POSSIBLE — IN OTHER WORDS, DON'T MOVE YOUR HANDS, ARMS, FEET OR HEAD MUCH WHILE WAITING FOR A PITCH. AND WHEN YOU SWING, THINK FULL EXTENSION OF THOSE ARMS, NOT JUST IN MEETING THE PITCH BUT ALSO IN THE FOLLOW-THROUGH.

By that time, McGwire had an option.

Former major-leaguer Marcel Lachemann had crossed paths with Carroll one day at a California Angels game. Knowing that Lachemann was the pitching coach at the University of Southern California, Carroll recommended he check out Carroll's big senior hurler. Lachemann obliged and, after watching McGwire pitch only three innings, confirmed he didn't need to see any more.

"I'm going to get the 'Old Man,'" Lachemann said.

Rod Dedeaux, the veteran head coach at USC, was the most respected name not only in college baseball but in amateur sports. For Dedeaux to show up at any high school game in the Southern California area was just a little short of a rock star or movie star mingling in public.

"Dedeaux came, he watched two or three innings with Mark pitching, and then Lachemann came over and said, 'Coach wants to talk to him after the game,'" Carroll said. While Dedeaux waited, he met John and Ginger McGwire and tried to convince them that Mark should accept a scholarship to USC. There were no other scholarship offers.

But there was the allure of pro ball. The Expos took care of that decision.

"I didn't really want to go to college," Mark said. "I wanted to play pro ball. Because it was a situation where it was either college or $8,500, I took college."

That turned out to be a great decision. His life took a decidedly different direction because of it.

1260

MLB | career walks: 1260

The 1983 USC media guide noted: "Pitching will be back to USC's standard of excellence. One of the main reasons ... is the return of sophomore starter McGwire."

Years later, Dedeaux said, "I still believe he was a definite major-league pitching prospect."

McGwire stood 6 feet 5 inches and 210 pounds, a lanky and somewhat imposing righthanded pitcher with a powerful fastball and good breaking ball. He pitched 20 games, most in relief, as a freshman and was second on the USC staff with a 3.04 earned-run average. McGwire also hit three home runs that season, but he really didn't have many chances to hit. No one worried about his hitting.

Not that people were shocked whenever McGwire hit a bomb. When USC assistant coach Marcel Lachemann first scouted him as a high school player, he reported back to Dedeaux that McGwire was quite a pitcher. But Lachemann also told USC hitting coach Ron Vaughn, just as an aside, "You've got to see this kid hit."

It didn't matter. McGwire wanted to be a pitcher, and Dedeaux said, "We knew we had a good one."

That loose arm, that smooth delivery, that strong desire – McGwire impressed all those who watched him pitch. McGwire wasn't one to boast about his abilities even then. He was shy, hard-working, uncomfortable with compliments or praise. The best part about playing baseball, McGwire thought, was just being on a team and having fun with the guys, that and the challenge of improving himself.

Scouts who saw him as a college freshman thought he already had a fastball suited for the major leagues and a curveball refined almost to that point. Said Brad Brink, a USC teammate who later reached the big leagues: "He threw really hard, had an incredible arm, a 90-plus mph fastball." Said Steve Bast, who played with McGwire in high school as well as at USC: "He wasn't 'Roger Clemens-overpowering,' but he threw hard and kept the ball down."

Sure enough, McGwire led the USC pitching staff with a 2.78 earned-run average his sophomore year. But McGwire wasn't really the pitching leader at USC, because he pitched only eight games as a sophomore.

> "He hit a popup against us one day that went so high, it was higher than the sun. **It was up there so high, all nine guys on our team called for it.**"
>
> RICH DONNELLY, COACH, COLORADO ROCKIES

He wasn't really a pitcher anymore. McGwire mostly played first base and proved it a good move. Try a .319 batting average, 59 RBIs in 53 games and a record 19 home runs on for size. That was an average of one homer for every 10 at-bats. McGwire went wild the next year, a junior and comfortable with his new baseball lifestyle. He broke his own USC record by hitting 32 home runs that season and became the school's career record-holder for homers with 54. Before he came along, no one in USC's storied baseball history had hit more than 32 career home runs.

What kind of talented pitcher would give up that position and instead choose a somewhat uncertain future as a hitter? "Two I can think of," Vaughn said years later, after he had left USC and taken a job as an Oakland scout. "Babe Ruth and Stan Musial."

So what happened between McGwire's freshman and sophomore years at Southern Cal? His life changed dramatically in the summer of 1982, in the somewhat unlikely setting of Alaska. The Alaska Summer League is one of the elite amateur programs for collegiate players, and McGwire went there to play for the Anchorage Glacier Pilots.

That team, as it turned out, came up short of first basemen for various reasons, so they had to look elsewhere on their roster in hopes of someone, anyone, to play the position. Their eyes stopped at McGwire's name on the pitching staff.

"And he hit the ball from the very first game," said Dick Lobdell, the team's radio play-by-play man that summer. "A week or two later, he finally got in to pitch and got shelled. He wasn't very impressive at all, so it was back to first base."

The Glacier Pilots' team record for batting average in a season was .409. In his first season, McGwire batted .403, hit 13 home runs and drove in 53 runs in a mere 44 games. He was just having fun, just learning how to hit. Heck, he was 19 and away from home in Southern California for the first extended time in his life. He missed his parents and brothers. He missed a girlfriend he had at the time. But none of the homer heroics went to his head.

"He was bright and articulate," Lobdell said. "The way I found out with Mark was he missed a couple games because he was hurt, and he came up and did color commentary on the radio with me. He was pretty good."

Vaughn, the USC assistant coach, happened to be an assistant coach with the Anchorage club as well. He knew McGwire had gone to Alaska to improve as a pitcher. But he secretly had planned to work with McGwire at the plate as well, to perhaps turn him into someone capable of doubling as a designated hitter. Vaughn helped McGwire eliminate his long swing, which made him prone to too many strikeouts. He got McGwire to lower his elbow and hands, shorten his stride, make his swing quicker through the strike zone. But no one, not even Vaughn, had an idea that McGwire would go to Alaska as a top pitching prospect and end up pitching very little, learning a new position and falling in love with the part of the game that involves swinging a bat.

"Somewhere along the line up there in Alaska," McGwire said, "it hit me, 'You know, I'd rather play every day than every fifth day.' Then, I started getting some hits. Ron Vaughn, who's one of my biggest mentors as a hitter, pretty much started me and taught me everything I needed to know."

There was one major problem: Dedeaux still valued McGwire as that major-league pitching prospect. "Rod totally resisted it until he saw the three-run homers I was hitting," McGwire said with a smile. "Then, he loved it."

The home runs were frequent and long. He once hit a batting-practice drive that shattered the windshield of a BMW parked past a left-field fence. Some wise guy wrote "Ouch" on the battered car. Dedeaux himself remembers one McGwire homer hit to left-center field at Arizona State in Tucson that cleared a large scoreboard and fell to earth "about nine miles from home plate." Later in the same game, another McGwire homer went so far into the darkness in right field that no one actually saw it touch down.

It wasn't just that he hit long home runs. He hit timely home runs. "He just knew ... when the game was on the line, it seemed like he always hit a home run or something," USC teammate Brad Brink said. "He was a clutch player, not just a home-run hitter. That's the sign of a great player. And we all knew he was a great player, even if he didn't know it about himself."

> **"** We didn't get to see Roger Maris set the record back in 1961.
>
> # Mark McGwire can be the record-breaker
>
> for our generation to look back on
> and remember the rest of our lives.**"**
>
> NEW YORK BASEBALL FAN MOISES CONCEPCION, WHO WAS 16
> WHEN HE WATCHED MCGWIRE PLAY AT SHEA STADIUM IN 1998

McGwire pitched in eight games as a sophomore and compiled a 3-1 record with a 2.78 ERA. But he had become a hitter, batting .319 with 19 homers and 59 RBIs in 53 games that season. As a junior, he turned into an All-American and one of the most dangerous hitters in college baseball history. He batted .387, drove in 80 runs in 67 games, had 20 doubles and 32 homers.

Clearly, McGwire would be a first-round draft pick after that junior season. "It's going to be tough to find another McGwire," Dedeaux said.

His teammates called him "Big Mac." When he was on the verge of becoming a rich young man in 1984, teammates started teasing him about it in a good-natured, almost admiring way. He was a star. They knew it − even if he didn't.

Before the draft in 1984, there was talk of the Mets choosing McGwire, but the Oakland Athletics ended up drafting him.

McGwire had no idea at the time that he would develop into a major-league power hitter. Frankly, he didn't give it much thought.

"I was too young," he remembered many years later. "I was just happy to be playing. Then, you always have the thing in the back of your mind: 'You know, I'm using an aluminum bat. How can you obviously say I'm a home run hitter?' Anybody can be a home run hitter with an aluminum bat. I don't think I accepted it."

seventy

MLB | single-season most home runs: 70

Everyone else was more than happy to place that expectation of power on McGwire's broad shoulders. He was tall and somewhat lean when he emerged from the college ranks – 6 feet 5 and about 225 pounds – but the Oakland Athletics drafted him with plans that McGwire would become a big-league home run hitter.

The United States Olympic Team wanted McGwire aboard for the same reason. Before he began his professional career, McGwire was the first baseman for Team USA in the 1984 Olympics played in Los Angeles. Baseball was just a demonstration sport that year, the first time it was included in the Olympics in any capacity, but the U.S. squad – made up of numerous future major-leaguers – took it seriously.

McGwire batted .359 with six homers and 26 runs batted in during the schedule leading up to the Olympics. Team USA won all three preliminary games and knocked off South Korea to reach the gold-medal game. With the ever-powerful Cuban team participating in the Soviet Union boycott of those Olympics, the United States met Japan with the first-ever baseball gold medal on the line and lost 6-3.

The experience left a lasting, marvelous impression on McGwire, even though he had only four hits in the games in Los Angeles. Once finished, though, he knew it was time to move on to the rest of his life.

Time to find out what kind of pro ballplayer he would be.

A tired McGwire – whose season had started in February as he embarked on a co-MVP season in the Pacific 10 Conference with USC and proceeded with the Olympics – joined the Modesto A's, a Single-A farm club of the Athletics that played in the California League. He batted .200 in 16 games. Batting 55 times, McGwire struck out 21 times, drew eight walks and hit just one home run. Not only was he trying to summon the energy to finish the long season, but he was using a wood bat for the first time as well.

"He had to make some adjustments," said former major-league player George Mitterwald, his manager at Modesto.

Not only on offense. The Athletics were loaded with good young talent throughout their minor-league system, including a catcher named Terry Steinbach, a strong outfielder named Jose Canseco and a promising first baseman named Rob Nelson. Oakland officials decided they wanted McGwire to learn to play third base, and the process began that fall in instructional league.

He struggled in the field the next year, but McGwire clearly had all the ability at the plate that the Athletics could want. He tied for the lead in the California League with 24 homers and 106 RBIs in 1985. Despite the defensive troubles, McGwire established what would become a career-long trademark: intensely hard work. He took countless ground balls every day, and he spent hours trying to become a hitter and not just a swinger.

All the work paid off in 1986. He opened the season with a promotion to Double-A Huntsville, Alabama, in the Southern League and needed only 55 games there before the Athletics decided he was ready for Triple-A. McGwire batted .303 with 10 homers and 53 RBIs with Huntsville, then compiled a .318 average with 13 home runs and 59 runs batted in during only 78 games while he played for Tacoma, Washington, in the Triple-A Pacific Coast League. He hit a home run in his first game and had at least one hit in 20 of his first 21 games with Tacoma. He wouldn't be there long.

On August 20, 1986, McGwire got the call from the Athletics. They wanted him in the big leagues. Was he ready?

"He just had a tremendous work ethic," said Keith Lieppman, then manager at Tacoma. "He realized that was going to pay off for him."

It already had.

MLB | single-season most hits: 161

From the beginning, McGwire found himself linked with the likes of Babe Ruth, Harmon Killebrew, Frank Howard and everyone else who hit baseballs high and deep and often over any fence a big-league team could build throughout the game's history.

Yet McGwire always has wanted to be a regular teammate, one of the 25 guys in a clubhouse, just another player who works hard. In 1997, he observed, "It's just been the last few years people have been writing more and more about home runs. People keep making a big deal about the Roger Maris thing whenever someone hits a bunch. But what does it mean when someone doesn't hit 61? Does that mean he failed?

"He is like the Empire State Building standing there with a bat in his hand. Words can't describe how good he is – to keep doing it day after day with the media pressure. I would have liked to see Ruth and him in the same era."

JIM THOME, CLEVELAND FIRST BASEMAN

"Nobody writes about how hard it is to hit a home run. It's the hardest thing to do in sports today. You can't try to do it."

But he did it from the start. Home-run hitters always have been great American heroes since Babe Ruth turned homers into the ultimate sports thrill in the 1920s. McGwire took his natural gifts, refined them with tireless work in the weight room and batting cages, discovered failure and had a rebirth – all with the Oakland Athletics.

1987 | a record 49 home runs as a rookie

49

In Oakland, Mac didn't have to be a leader. And that was good, considering McGwire arrived as a private, shy rookie in 1987 who didn't want to be a celebrity, just a working man like his buddies at the time – police officers, comedians, golfers.

Said former Oakland coach Jim Lefebvre: "He had an attitude you'd like to copy and distribute to all young players."

McGwire listened to the veterans, admired them, didn't want to upstage them but rather liked to be a complementary player. Manager Tony La Russa called him the best on those Oakland teams at moving a runner from second base with a ball hit to the right side or with a hit. And he's been an excellent defensive first baseman from the day he arrived in the big leagues.

Mac valued his life away from the ballpark. From the beginning, that involved being a father. Mark had married his college sweetheart while in the minor leagues, and soon they were expecting their first child. McGwire set the major-league record for a rookie with 49 home runs and on the final day of the season had a chance to become the first rookie ever to reach the 50-homer plateau. Instead, he chose to beg out of that season finale so he could be with his then-wife for the birth of son Matthew. From that day forward, he listed Matthew as "definitely" the most important aspect of his life.

McGwire actually was promoted to the majors on August 20, 1986. He had split his season at Double-A and Triple-A in the minors and had combined totals of a .311 batting average, 23 homers and 112 RBIs when called to the big leagues. After his first two days in the majors were rained out in Baltimore, he got his first major-league hit on August 24 in a game against the New York Yankees, with legendary Tommy John on the pitcher's mound. His first major-league home run came on August 25, when the Athletics were playing the Detroit Tigers at historic Tiger Stadium. His homer came off pitcher Walt Terrell.

Frankly, his initial steps in the majors didn't go well during the end of that 1986 season. He batted .189 and had three homers in 53 at-bats. His defense at third base, where he committed six errors, indicated he needed to find a new position. But those around him could see McGwire was something special.

"The only thing he lacks is speed," teammate Jose Canseco observed then. "But power hitters don't need speed. They just need to be able to trot around the bases."

While at Southern Cal, McGwire had developed the kind of swing that produced that power – hands lowered, a pigeon-toed crouch, a short and compact swing with incredible extension of his arms in his follow-through. He also had started lifting weights diligently and in fact had fallen in love with that aspect of training.

"What helps Mark is that he is 6-5 and 230 pounds," Athletics hitting coach Bob Watson said his rookie year. "He doesn't have to hit the ball on the screws to hit it out. He can hit the ball on the end of the bat and still get home runs or base hits."

Back at first base, Mac showed just that in 1987 when he was named the AL Rookie of the Year. He was only the second man voted that award unanimously by the Baseball Writers' Association of America. The vote was partly for his 49 homers, which tied Cubs outfielder Andre Dawson for most in the majors. The vote also recognized that McGwire had set the big-league record for a rookie (the record had been 38) and broken Reggie Jackson's Oakland record. Talk about him someday challenging Roger Maris' single-season record of 61 homers surfaced at the All-Star break, when McGwire had 33 home runs and 68 RBIs.

"We're just so proud.

If I had buttons on my shirt, they'd be popping."

GINGER McGWIRE, MARK'S MOM

"When he was hitting a home run every seven at-bats and people were saying he'd hit 70," teammate Terry Steinbach said then, "he'd say, 'Forget it. Don't be ridiculous.'"

Although McGwire didn't hit as many as 49 homers in a season again until 1996, he clearly was one of the top power hitters the next three years. He averaged 35 home runs and 101 RBIs from 1988 through 1990. His batting average declined steadily, but McGwire couldn't be selfish about that. He was producing runs, and the Athletics became a powerhouse in baseball. They reached the World Series in each of those three seasons, with McGwire hitting well against Boston and Toronto in the American League playoffs the first two years.

130

MLB | single-season most runs: 130

The ultimate moment came in 1989, when the A's defeated cross-bay rivals the San Francisco Giants to win the World Championship. That year, the World Series was interrupted for several days while the San Francisco Bay area dealt with a massive earthquake that struck just as the teams were preparing for Game Three at Candlestick Park.

For McGwire, his stay at Oakland was both wonderful and depressing. He went through almost everything a major-leaguer can experience with the Athletics. Cheered and jeered. Winning the American League home run title. Being named to nine All-Star teams, taking part in three teams that won the AL pennant, winning the World Series.

Suffering through back and foot injuries that wouldn't let him on the field for even a fourth of his team's games. Going through a divorce. Watching his teammates leave one by one through trades and free agency because Oakland's owners couldn't afford to pay them, then seeing manager Tony La Russa leave as well.

In 1991, McGwire batted .201 and fretted considerably. He was battling through back problems that had begun a few years earlier. Although he was able to play 154 games, he wasn't up to the standards he had set for himself, with only 22 homers and 75 RBIs.

"It was frustrating trying to climb out of a hole that just got deeper and deeper," he said. On a long drive home that winter from Las Vegas to his home in Southern California, McGwire kept the music off in his car and thought. He thought about his life, both on and off the field, and realized he didn't have the answers on how to clean things up. So he decided to see a therapist.

"It would have been easy for me to hide and put my head in a hole and sit down and sulk and say, 'Poor me,'" McGwire said some years later. "But I wanted to turn my life around."

The difficult season taught McGwire to take care of his mind and his body, to know what he needed to do both in the offseason and during summer to keep his back from limiting his performance. Dedicated weight training helped him add about 20 pounds of muscle, with the help of his weight-trainer brother J.J. McGwire. Mark looked like a new man, with 42 homers that finished second to Juan Gonzalez's 43 – despite McGwire's missing 20 games with a muscle strain during the season.

He boosted his batting average from the previous season to .268 and finished among the league leaders in several categories. On June 10, he hit his 22nd home run of the season in Milwaukee, which gave him 200 career homers. Only Ralph Kiner, Babe Ruth, Harmon Killebrew and Eddie Mathews had reached the 200 mark in fewer at-bats. At the All-Star Game, he won the Home Run Derby by hitting 12 out.

The Athletics won the American League West Division title for the fourth time in five seasons, and McGwire hit a home run off Toronto's Jack Morris in his first at-bat of the playoffs. But he had only two more hits the rest of the series, and Oakland failed to reach the World Series.

That was the beginning of McGwire's miseries. He played a mere 74 combined games in the 1993-94 seasons, hitting nine homers each year. It actually forced him to ponder retirement.

A heel injury limited him to only two pinch-hitting appearances after May 14 in 1993, when he played only 27 games. He underwent surgery that September. That allowed him to show up healthy at spring training in 1994, but a stress fracture in his left heel put him on the disabled list for 6 weeks during the first half of the season. He reinjured the heel in late July and needed surgery again.

A players' strike delayed the start of the 1995 season. And he missed a bunch of other games for several reasons – being beaned by a David Cone pitch, suffering a bruised foot, feeling the recurrence of his back problem. But McGwire had undergone a complete metamorphosis. He was mostly a healthy man, a stronger man, a man who enjoyed the mental aspects of baseball and simply appreciated the game better than ever before.

McGwire responded to his new baseball life with vigor: 39 homers and 90 RBIs in only 104 games in 1995, then a career-high .312 batting average with 52 homers and 113 RBIs in 1996.

Baseball Tips for Young Players:
CATCHING

FOR A CATCHER, THE MOST IMPORTANT TRAITS ARE TO HAVE THE TRUST AND CONFIDENCE OF YOUR PITCHER. THAT MAKES COMMUNICATION WITH HIM VITAL. MAKE SURE YOU ARE THINKING THE SAME WAY ABOUT WHAT HE IS TRYING TO DO ON EVERY PITCH. IF YOU ARE TALKING OPENLY AND HONESTLY, THEN HE WILL BE MORE OPEN TO YOUR SUGGESTIONS AND OBSERVATIONS. HE CAN HAVE MORE CONFIDENCE IN YOU IF HE NOTICES HOW HARD YOU ARE WORKING ON HIS BEHALF. THAT CAN INCLUDE BLOCKING BALLS IN THE DIRT. MOVE FREELY AND QUICKLY FROM SIDE TO SIDE AND MAKE SURE YOUR GLOVE IS DOWN, COVERING THE SPACE BETWEEN YOUR KNEES, RATHER THAN STABBING AT THE BALL ON THE OUTSIDES OF YOUR LEGS WITH YOUR GLOVE.

The next year, talk of pursuing the Roger Maris record emerged again. Through the first four months of the season, he had 34 home runs and 81 RBIs. He was clearly one of the dominant players in baseball.

Yet by the time the 1997 season came around, the Athletics were a shadow of their former selves. McGwire was the entire show. He didn't like it. "I don't want to be on a loser," Mac said. "I'm tired of losing." He wanted to be a teammate again. He wanted to be part of a winner.

"All the attention on home runs takes away from what the purpose is, to play baseball," McGwire said. "This is a team sport, not an individual sport. There is no purpose in picking out one player to focus on. You don't play this game for attention, you play because God gave you the ability to. You play for fun."

Mac couldn't see any fun in the near future in Oakland. With his free agency looming, that winter McGwire made it clear he probably would sign with another team and thus the Athletics felt compelled to try to make a trade.

The Athletics sent McGwire to St. Louis at the trading deadline – July 31, 1997 – in exchange for major-league reliever T.J. Mathews and minor-league pitching prospects Blake Stein and Eric Ludwick. Mac would be rejoining La Russa and Walt Jocketty, the Cardinals' general manager who engineered the trade and had known him in Oakland years earlier.

No one really expected McGwire to stay in St. Louis, of course. His son was back in Southern California. He had a home there, had lived in California essentially his entire life, had been a part of the American League his entire career.

Jocketty was convinced that something special was about to unfold. "When he sees what a quality baseball environment it is [in St. Louis] – with the organization, with the stadium we have and most of all the fans – I think when he gets there, he's going to be surprised how great it really is," Jocketty said at the time of the deal.

"It's going to be a challenge," McGwire said at the time. "And to tell you the truth, I think that's what I need. ... I'll just keep doing the things I've always done and try to put up some good numbers for the Cardinals."

MLB | single-season most walks: 162

162

1998 | hit record-distance 545-foot home run

But he never had thought about playing anywhere
other than the American League and in California, where
he could be near his son and parents and friends.

He tried to keep an open mind.

"I think you come to a crossroads in your life where change is good for you,"
McGwire said. "And I've come to those crossroads."

McGwire figured he would play out the last two months of the 1997 season with
the Cardinals, then field contract offers from other teams. And the Cardinals didn't
exactly look like a winner. He stated he truly wanted to get back to the World Series
before he retired, and the Cardinals seemed far from that level.

The Cardinals were losing games at an alarming rate and needed what
McGwire had to offer. Although he struggled to hit initially, he drew huge
crowds every day from the beginning, in Philadelphia on August 1.

The reception was intense in
St. Louis. Several thousand fans
showed up two hours before each
game to watch him take batting
practice, and they applauded
every move he made. He rewarded
the fans with more power than
St. Louis ever had witnessed.

"I've never seen the reaction to anybody that I've seen to this guy.

I wouldn't even say Ozzie Smith was worshiped the way Mark McGwire is."

TOM PAGNOZZI, FORMER CARDINALS CATCHER

For instance, on August 13 he cracked two homers, with one of them traveling 455 feet. Exactly three weeks later, he hit a 504-foot home run off White Sox pitcher Jaime Navarro, the first homer that ever measured longer than 500 feet at Busch. "He hits home runs like we hit singles," catcher Tom Pagnozzi said.

On September 10, he hit his 16th home run since joining the Cardinals. Added to the 34 he had hit with the Athletics before the trade, McGwire had a total of 50 for the season. That made him only the second player in the history of major-league baseball to hit 50 or more home runs for two successive seasons. Babe Ruth was the other, and McGwire said "it blows me away" to be mentioned in the same sentence as Ruth.

fifty

1997 | hit 50 or more home runs in 2 successive seasons

One of the most significant days in the history of St. Louis sports arrived on September 17, 1997. Walt Jocketty, the Cardinals' general manager, had been right. The tradition, the young talent in the organization, the atmosphere – it all won over McGwire's heart. At a news conference that afternoon, he announced that he had signed a three-year contract with an option to play a fourth year for the team as well.

McGwire also revealed he was pledging $1 million a year to establish The Mark McGwire Foundation to fight sexual and physical abuse of children. He wiped away tears as he explained the decision was because of a close friend who had suffered such abuse. And from another close friend who worked with abused children, he heard stories that wouldn't let him stand idly by. "I'm at a time in my life when I want to help them out," McGwire said. "... I don't think there's enough help out there for these young kids."

But the emotion of that day was far from finished. The Cardinals had a game that night at Busch Stadium against the Los Angeles Dodgers. In McGwire's first at-bat after signing the new contract, 27,157 fans rose to their feet as they waited for pitcher Ramon Martinez to throw the ball to the big redheaded slugger. McGwire blasted the fifth pitch 517 feet, the longest hit ever recorded at the ballpark. It landed in the upper deck, over the left-field scoreboard and gave him 18 home runs in only 48 days wearing a Cardinals uniform.

"I don't think it was too hard to fall in love with St. Louis," McGwire said. "It makes me float every time I come to the ballpark and play in front of these fans."

1998

He finished that 1997 season with 58 home runs – 34 with Oakland, 24 with the Cardinals. He finished the year with a flourish, as he hit two homers on the second-to-last day and one on the final day of the schedule. No righthanded batter ever had hit as many as 58 homers in a season.

Frequently throughout the 1998 season, McGwire would tell reporters, "I'm just a normal person." He had a difficult time convincing anyone of that, however. The homers kept coming at such a torrid pace that he certainly didn't appear normal.

But, McGwire insisted, his life and achievements should stand as lessons for all those people who really do consider themselves average, regular people who know heartache and difficulties as they try to fulfill their goals. What kind of people needed to pay attention to him?

"If you believe in dreams, if you believe in yourself as far as climbing mountains, busting through the walls when you have adversity," McGwire once said during the course of making baseball history. "My God, I've had enough adversity in my life, enough in my professional life. It would have been easy for me to turn around and never be heard from again. But I decided to bust through these walls, to conquer it. ... it has not been easy professionally and personally to get to where I'm at. I'm a perfect example of the person who is normal that can conquer things if they dream and believe in themselves."

He reported to Jupiter, Florida, for his first spring training with the Cardinals in February 1998. When he arrived, people wanted to know if this was the year someone finally would hit 61 home runs as Maris of the Yankees did in 1961. McGwire seemed the obvious choice for the attention. He had fallen only three short the year before. His name already had been linked with that of Babe Ruth and every other slugger who ever hit a ball 500 feet. People had been mentioning McGwire in the same sentence as Maris since he was a rookie 11 years earlier.

What would it feel like to round the bases after hitting a 62nd home run? He wouldn't say. Couldn't say. Too far off. If anyone had 50 home runs by the first of September, then he had a chance. Short of that, it just didn't make sense to speculate.

He didn't like being the only name considered. What about Ken Griffey Jr. or Juan Gonzalez or several others? He saw plenty of players who had to be considered just as likely as he was to break the record.

But four games into the season, McGwire already had separated from the pack. He hit a homer in each game. The drama was palpable from the first day, when he went to bat in a scoreless game and whacked a grand slam that helped the Cardinals to a 6-0 victory.

1998 | hit season home run 61 on his dad's 61st birthday

61

Soon, almost every newspaper in the United States was keeping daily track of his exploits. There usually was a chart showing how many home runs Roger Maris had on that date en route to his 61 in 1961 and how many Babe Ruth had on his way to his 60 home runs in 1927, and right beside it was McGwire's picture, his current home run total and a projection of what he would end up with.

"I play with pressure every day," said McGwire, who found more and more reporters wanting to talk with him and thousands of fans leaving disappointed if he didn't hit a home run in a game.

But he rarely disappointed them. Historic moments arrived with increasing regularity.

His 13th home run of the 1998 season gave him 400 career homers, making him only the 26th man in baseball history to reach that level – and no one had done it in fewer at-bats than McGwire. By the All-Star break, talk of the Maris record falling was feverish, since McGwire had 37 home runs already.

By July 11, though, McGwire had gone seven games without a home run. Then he received a boost from Matt McGwire, his 10-year-old son, who was in town to visit his dad and serve as Cardinals batboy. Just before the game that day, Mark had Matt kiss his bat – and Mark belted a home run in the 11th inning to knock off the Houston Astros. The next day, he hit two home runs for a 6-4 victory, giving him 40 homers for the season. That made him only the third player in Cardinals history to get to the 40 plateau.

No one in baseball history had gotten to 40 home runs in one season any faster than McGwire, who needed only 281 at-bats, in the 90th game of the season.

"Forty is a nice number," McGwire said. " ... [But] I still have a lot of work ahead of me."

He soon reached No. 42, matching the total the great Rogers Hornsby hit for the Cardinals in 1922. In late July, he stroked No. 43, which tied the Cardinals' single-season team record that Johnny Mize had held since 1940. By then, Mac was swatting alongside Chicago Cubs slugger Sammy Sosa, who never really had been mentioned as a possibility to challenge Maris' record since he never had hit as many as 40 homers in any one season. But Sosa hit 20 home runs in June alone, and suddenly he was right with McGwire. Together, they generated more attention among the media than anyone ever had seen before.

On August 7, McGwire and the Cardinals arrived in St. Louis to play Sosa and the Cubs. Mac had 45 homers. Sammy had 43. They were competitors in a race neither really wanted to acknowledge. They joked with each other, though, and each seemed too friendly to be driven to finish with more homers than the other, much less reach Maris' mark first.

They respected each other. Sosa said: "I'm going to watch him [take batting practice] because he's the man. I can't wait for it. I've never seen a human being hit the ball like that."

McGwire said, "Why can't we have friendships? That's the beauty of the game. Here are two guys from two different countries that have great sportsmanship and really admire each other, really pull for each other."

By the time the Cardinals went to Chicago to play the Cubs for games on August 18 and August 19, each man had 47 homers. Neither one went deep in the first game. The next day, Sosa moved ahead for the first time, when he hit his 48th of the season in the fifth inning. But that lead lasted only 58 minutes, as McGwire hit his own No. 48 in the eighth inning to tie the game 6-6 and then belted No. 49 in the 10th inning of an 8-6 victory.

"I don't usually get too excited," McGwire said. "But I did today."

That was the beginning of a phenomenal run of excitement. Including that game, McGwire hit 15 home runs in a span of 22 games.

He hit two more homers – one in each game of a doubleheader against the Mets at New York's Shea Stadium – to reach 51. That made him the first player in major-league history to hit 50 homers in three consecutive seasons. And since it was only August 20, he admitted he finally had a chance to break the record. Two days later, he hit No. 52 in Pittsburgh. "I'm getting my second wind," McGwire said. "I'm feeling really good now."

1998 | broke Roger Maris' single-season home run record with 62

> " I can't say I want it to be broken. ...
> [But] it would be nice for Roger to see this.
> # I know he'd get
> # a kick out of it. "
>
> PATRICIA MARIS EARLY IN 1998 ON THE POSSIBILITY
> OF MCGWIRE BREAKING HER HUSBAND'S RECORD

McGwire hit No. 54 against the Florida Marlins, a 509-foot shot that wasn't mammoth – like the 545-footer he had hit off Florida pitcher Livan Hernandez earlier in the season – but was notable because he could hit a ball that far so late in the season. He still wasn't impressed by the distance of his homers and was only slightly impressed by their frequency. He could trade them for something having to do with his team: "Quite a few more wins," he said.

But the focus was on McGwire, not his Cardinals teammates, for the rest of the season. He hit Nos. 56 and 57 in Florida on September 1 and then Nos. 58 and 59 in Florida the next day. Sosa had hit his 56th on the same night, but McGwire called that a coincidence. "If the record is meant to happen, then it's going to happen," Mac said. "I'll just do my best."

He wanted to set the record in front of the fans in St. Louis. Amazingly, he did so during a relatively brief home stand.

■ September 5, 1998, against the Reds at Busch Stadium. McGwire hit the 60th homer of his season off rookie Dennis Reyes. That matched Ruth's total of 1927. "Babe Ruth," McGwire said, savoring the name. "It is almost – you are almost speechless when people put your name alongside his name."

■ September 7, 1998, against the Cubs at Busch. McGwire belted a pitch from Mike Morgan 430 feet for homer No. 61, a perfect 61st birthday gift for his father, John McGwire. "Now," Mark said, "we are one swing away."

Mark had hoped his son would be there to share the excitement with him, but Matt was still on a flight from California, arriving in St. Louis less than 45 minutes before the first pitch was thrown. Matt wasn't at the ballpark when the game began. "I didn't see him there in the top of the first inning," Mark said. "Then, when I went into the hole to get my bat, there he is. I told him I loved him, gave him a kiss, next thing I knew I saw him at home plate. What a wonderful feeling a father could have."

■ September 8, 1998, against the Cubs at St. Louis. The day he never will forget turned out to be more special than he ever could have imagined back in spring training. On the final day of the home stand, McGwire gave Cardinals fans a thrill they never would forget by swatting No. 62.

Hitting a home run against a major-league pitcher is not easy. If it was, then everyone would put in the long hours of weight training in the offseason and muscle up to look like McGwire, then assault the record books the way he did. As it is, only he and Sosa have been able to move into the 60-homer range. Sosa finished that 1998 season with 66. McGwire slumped ever so slightly after hitting No. 62, then finished the season on a tear again. His final touch came on the last day of the season. Seventy. No. 70. A place no player ever had gone before.

seventy

1998 | hit 70 home runs

"I can't believe I did it. Can you?" McGwire said. "It's absolutely amazing. It blows me away. I think it's going to take longer for this whole season to sink in. I can't wait to get home and look at the tapes and read the magazines and read the newspaper articles, and let that sink in about what I did about hitting 62. But reaching the 70 plateau, I think it's going to take a little bit longer."

He tried to get away from it all that winter. He tried to relax. But it wasn't easy: McGwire had become the most recognizable, most sought-after figure in all of sports.

Trying to take a vacation in a place where he could find some peace and anonymity, McGwire went to Australia – and people noticed him. He accepted only a handful of the offers that came along for commercials, interviews and appearances. McGwire's offseason is important to him, since it's an opportunity to spend time with his son and Matt's friends. They play video games, see movies, just hang out after school. He misses that most of the year.

But the offseason also gives him an opportunity to relax his mind, to not think about baseball for a few months, and thus return fresh for the next season. Try as he did all that winter, McGwire couldn't completely avoid thoughts of 1998. The mental fatigue and attention from media and fans had taken a toll. When he showed up for spring training in 1999, he already felt worn out.

1999 | **first player to hit at least 50 home runs in 4 consecutive seasons**

Yet he waged another friendly homer battle with Sosa that summer and still found a way to prevail. Sosa finished that 1999 season with 63 home runs. McGwire hit 65, making him the first man in baseball history to hit at least 50 home runs in four consecutive years. He also reached the 500-homer level in his career, the first man to reach 400 and 500 in successive seasons and putting him in some truly exclusive company. That gave him a record 135 homers in back-to-back years.

"I think what I've done this year is maybe more impressive than what I did last year, considering ... the expectations people have for me now," McGwire said.

He truly had become a modern-day Babe Ruth. Because of his sacrifices and ability to overcome adversity, because of the time he put into honing his skills physically and mentally, because he never gave up, Mark McGwire will be linked forever to the home run and to No. 70.

Baseball Tips for Young Players: LONG TOSS

PLAY CATCH, ESPECIALLY LONG TOSS, AS OFTEN AS POSSIBLE. EVEN 15 MINUTES A DAY CAN MAKE A TREMENDOUS DIFFERENCE NOT ONLY IN PREVENTING ARM INJURIES BUT IN BUILDING THE KIND OF ARM STRENGTH THAT MANY MODERN PLAYERS LACK. THAT WILL COME IN HANDY ESPECIALLY FOR PLAYERS WHO WANT TO PLAY THE POSITIONS MOST IN DEMAND: THIRD BASEMEN, PITCHERS AND CATCHERS.

"The magnitude of 70 – obviously, it's a huge number," he said. "But you know, if you put your mind to something, it'll happen. I think [the record will] stand for a while. I know how grueling it is to do what I've done this year. Will it be broken some day? Could be. I don't know if I want to break my own record. I think I'd just rather leave it as it is."

Still, Mark says he would trade it all for a chance to play in a World Series with the St. Louis Cardinals. He doesn't like so much attention focused on just one player. He would prefer it spread around. He would prefer to win.

But that is likely to come for Mark McGwire before he retires. His life story seems to be about happy endings.

The Oakland Athletics hired Tony La Russa as their manager on July 1, 1986. Less than eight weeks later, on August 22, the A's promoted slugging infielder Mark McGwire to the major leagues for the first time. The two men have experienced many moments of glory and disappointment together ever since.

McGwire quietly convinced La Russa that he could be a star someday, as the manager watched McGwire during spring training in 1987, McGwire's first with Oakland as a major-leaguer and coincidentally the last big-league spring training for future Hall-of-Famer Reggie Jackson.

"Mark worked as hard as Reggie," La Russa once said. "Reggie had set a goal for himself to work harder than anybody in camp, and Mark stayed right with him. That's when I knew we had something special.

"I've been impressed since the first day of spring training. He came there and had to play his way on the team, and he's earned everything he's gotten. He's got good ability, and he's kept his wits about him. He's got a chance to be a very productive hitter because he uses the whole field. He's got a very compact stroke, the ball jumps off his bat, and, if he keeps applying himself, he's got a lot of ways to drive in a run. There's a lot of pitches he can handle. You can't stack the defense against him. You can't pitch him one way."

Shortly after La Russa was named Cardinals manager before the 1996 season, he often would discuss the best players of the American League. McGwire always was the first name he would mention, and not just because of his ability to hit home runs.

"He's a much better defensive first baseman and all-round player than anyone ever has given him credit for," La Russa said. "He's a very good base runner and just understands the game so well. Mark will do whatever it takes to help win – hit a sacrifice fly, move a runner over, anything. That's the best thing about him. He's just a great teammate and really wants to win. ...

"The one thing that he does that's the most impressive thing he does is talk to the other guys about the right way to be a professional winning player. He'll go to them and talk to them about things like taking a pitch when the team is behind, playing through minor injuries, hitting to the opposite field. And he likes to talk to, teach, and really get involved with the young players."

La Russa truly didn't think he ever would manage McGwire again. He thought that even if Mac left Oakland one day, he would probably

look at him. I mean, how do you look at someone who has just hit 70 home runs?!"

La Russa watched how McGwire handled all the attention in 1998 and 1999. He understands his first baseman and feels impressed at each twist and turn, both by his performances on the field and off.

"I think he likes the limelight. I just don't think he likes talking about himself. I think he likes the limelight of going to bat in the ninth inning with the game on the line.

"There was a popular, wrong theory going around, that the home run race between Mark and Sammy Sosa was not nearly as exciting the second time around. But there was a lot of attention to what they were doing. It definitely had a luster. Maybe not as brilliant, but I give them more credit for the second year than the first year. It's human nature after something like that to sit back and smell the roses. They didn't do that. They kept trying to do more. I know for Mark, all he wants to do is his best to help his team win every day. That's what drives him. That hasn't changed about him and never will.

"... We never take anything he does or anything he is for granted. You don't want to. You want to savor it all, appreciate it. I'm not surprised by anything he does any more. It's just been special to watch it all happen. ... Fans need to come out and watch him play. He won't be around forever. So you're going to want to bring your kids out and be able to say one day that you saw one of the greatest ever get to play baseball, because that's what Mark McGwire is – one of the greatest ever to play the game."

prefer to stay in the American League or remain in California because he would want to see his son, Matt, as often as possible. Besides, La Russa said, acquiring someone as good as McGwire would cost the Cardinals too much in a trade.

Once the Cardinals were able to acquire Mac from Oakland in July 1997, La Russa had a hunch fans would convince him to stay. But he had no idea what chapters in history would unfold. La Russa didn't enjoy at all the fact that the Cardinals finished well back in the National League Central Division race in 1998, but he was thrilled to watch one of his favorite players and people become the greatest single-season home-run hitter of all time.

And by the end, La Russa felt almost as drained and awed by it all as anyone. After the final game of the season, the manager considered what had just happened and said, "I'm glad we don't have to come back for another game tomorrow. I don't know if I could

GAME-DAY routine

WHEN THE CARDINALS PLAY AN EVENING HOME GAME, HERE'S WHAT MARK McGWIRE'S DAY LOOKS LIKE:

Mid-afternoon Arrive at Busch Stadium, often earlier than most of his teammates. Spend time, maybe a half-hour, lifting weights in the team's weight-training facility near the home team's clubhouse. Receive treatment on his back and occasionally his legs from Cardinals trainer Barry Weinberg. Hit off a batting tee and with soft pitching tosses from hitting coach Mike Easler in the indoor batting cage. Read a little, eat a light meal from the food room that is attached to the clubhouse, make phone calls to various friends, talk with teammates, conduct interviews with some reporters.

4:30 p.m. Head to the field to go through the regular stretching routine with the other players in the Cardinals' starting lineup that day. Field several dozen ground balls at first base.

5:10 p.m. Sign autographs at the far end of the Cardinals' dugout.

5:25 p.m. Begin batting practice at the outdoor cage on the field. Usually, Mac will bunt the first pitch and then take 8 to 10 swings in his first round. He will take turns hitting with three other teammates, with each player gradually taking fewer swings each time they step into the cage. By the time he is finished, McGwire will have hit 22 to 25 pitches.

5:50 p.m. Clear the field and head back to the clubhouse. With game time approaching, McGwire starts to focus on that day's pitcher and what he expects to see from him. He will spend most of the final hour putting on his game jersey, talking with teammates and preparing his mind for the game.

7:10 p.m. First pitch. Usually, that means McGwire is starting at first base for the Cardinals and batting either third or fourth in the lineup.

After the game Lift weights for a brief time, receive more treatment from the trainers on his back, eat a light meal. Usually following a shower, McGwire will talk with reporters about that night's game if he is needed, then dress and head out for a meal with some teammates. He often is one of the last players to leave the clubhouse.